Math in Focus®

Singapore Math®
by Marshall Cavendish

Student Book
Kindergarten Ⓑ
Part 1

Author
Dr. Pamela Sharpe

U.S. Consultants
Andy Clark and Patsy F. Kanter

Marshall Cavendish
Education

U.S. Distributor

**Houghton
Mifflin
Harcourt**

COMMON
CORE

© 2012 Marshall Cavendish International (Singapore) Private Limited
© 2014 Marshall Cavendish Education Pte Ltd

Published by Marshall Cavendish Education
Times Centre, 1 New Industrial Road, Singapore 536196
Customer Service Hotline: (65) 6213 9444
US Office Tel: (1-914) 332 8888 | Fax: (1-914) 332 8882
E-mail: tmesales@mceducation.com
Website: www.mceducation.com

Distributed by
Houghton Mifflin Harcourt
222 Berkeley Street
Boston, MA 02116
Tel: 617-351-5000
Website: www.hmheducation.com/mathinfocus

Second edition 2012

Math in Focus® Kindergarten B Part 1
ISBN 978-0-547-62524-9

Printed in China

13 14 15 16   1401   19 18 17 16
4500592253   B C D E

Contents

Contents

Solid and Flat Shapes

Lesson 1 Solid Shapes

Which shape is it? Color.

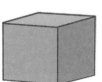

Match.

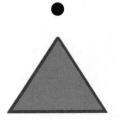

Pair.

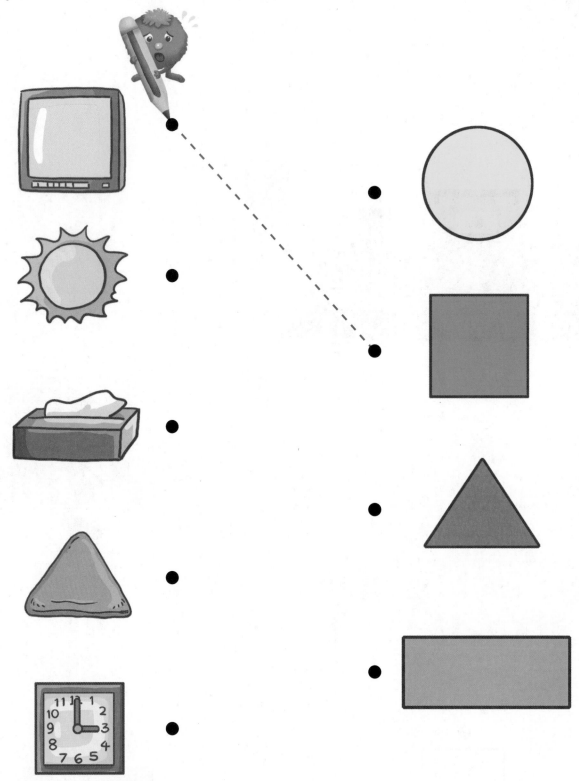

Draw.

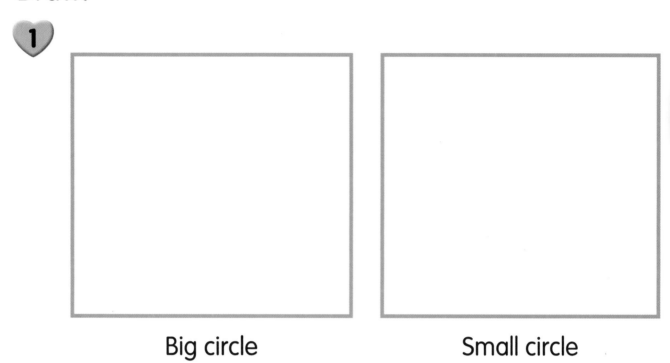

1

Big circle

Small circle

2

Small square

Big square

3

Big triangle

Small triangle

4

Small rectangle

Big rectangle

5

Big hexagon

Small hexagon

Color the squares red. Color the rectangles green. Color the circles yellow. Color the triangles blue. Color the hexagons brown.

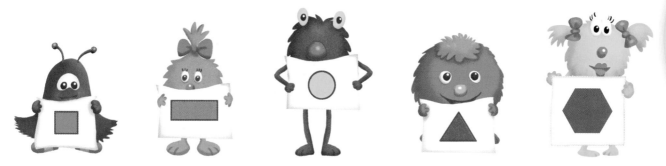

Lesson 5 Shape Patterns
Complete the pattern.

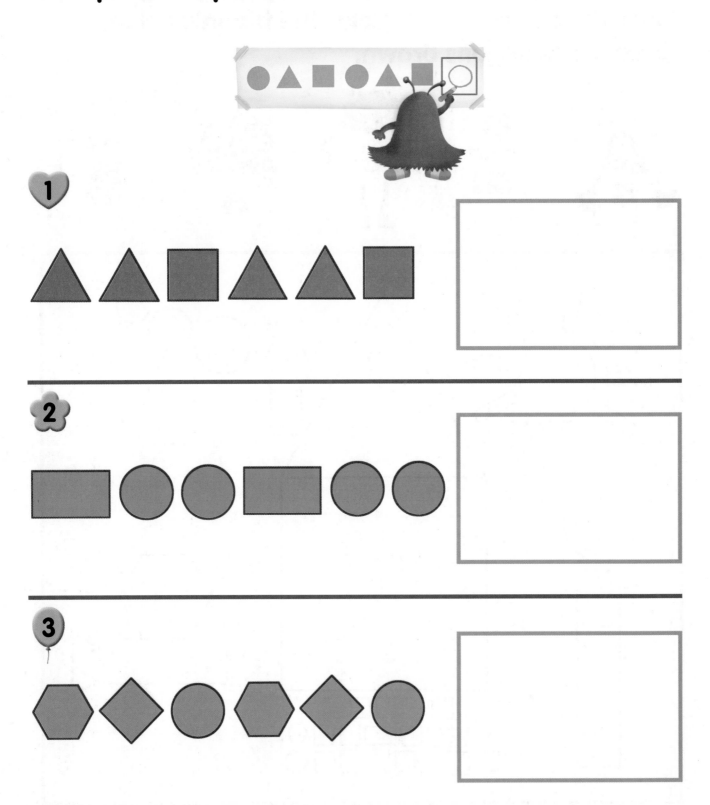

1

2

3

Lesson **1** **Counting by 2s**

Count and write.

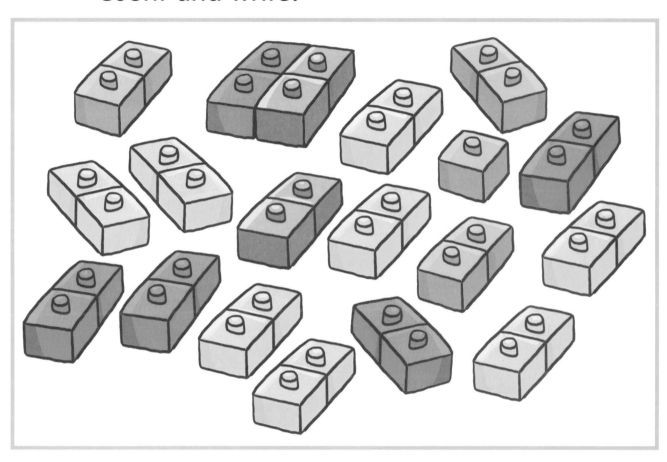

Circle the groups of 5 ants.

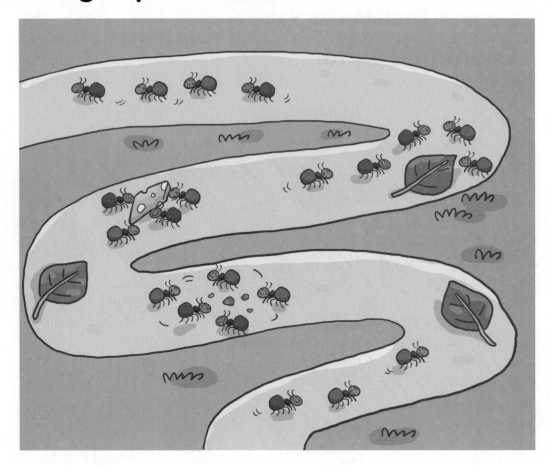

Make the tally.

How many? Count and circle.

 1

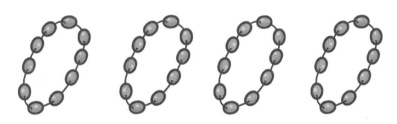

40   14   50

 2

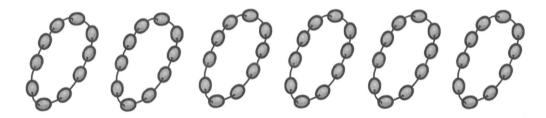

16   80   60

 3

11   100   90

Circle groups of 10. Then, count and circle.

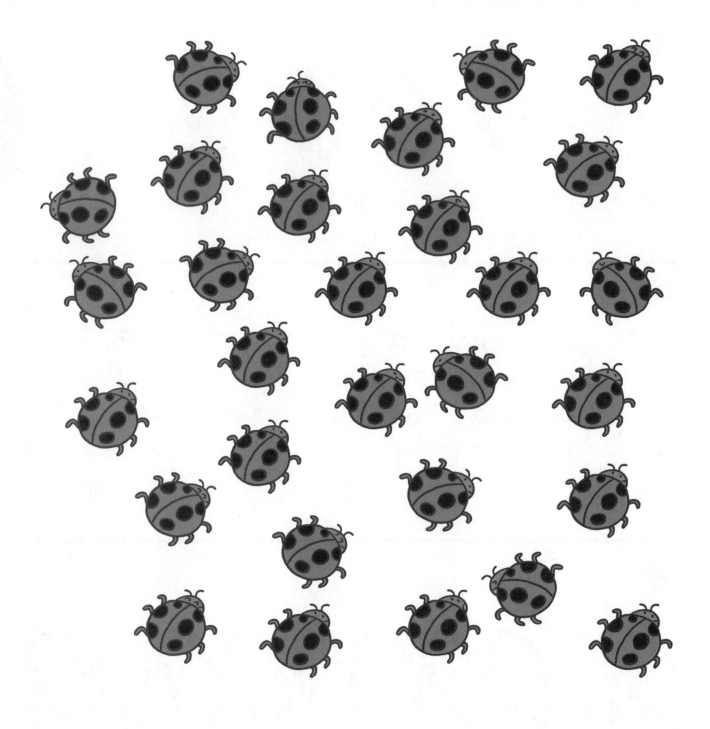

How many?   20   30   40

Read and color.

42

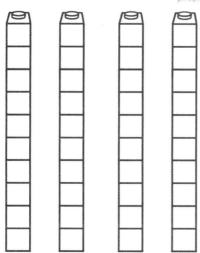

2

37

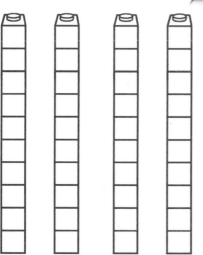

How many? Count and circle.

1

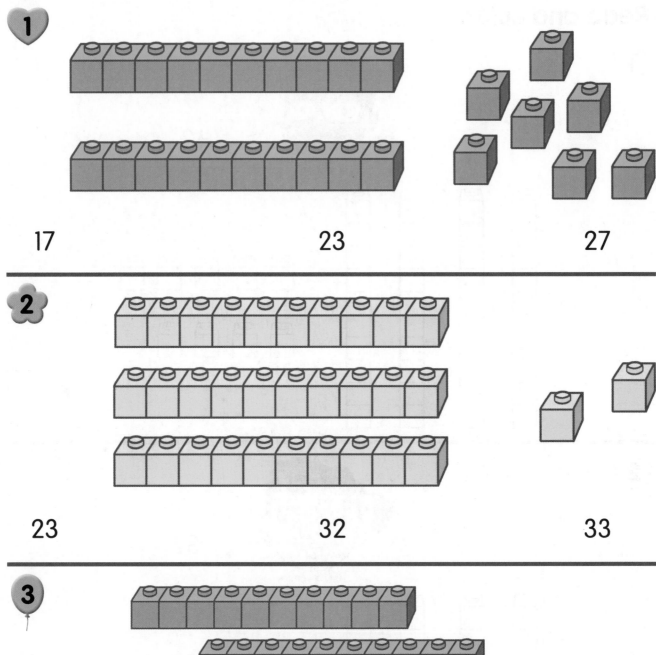

17 23 27

2

23 32 33

3

40 44 30

Complete the sequence. Circle the missing number.

1

20, 21, ___, 23

24   22   32

2

39, ___, 41, 42

38   30   40

3

27, 28, 29, ___

26   40   30

How many? Count and circle.

1

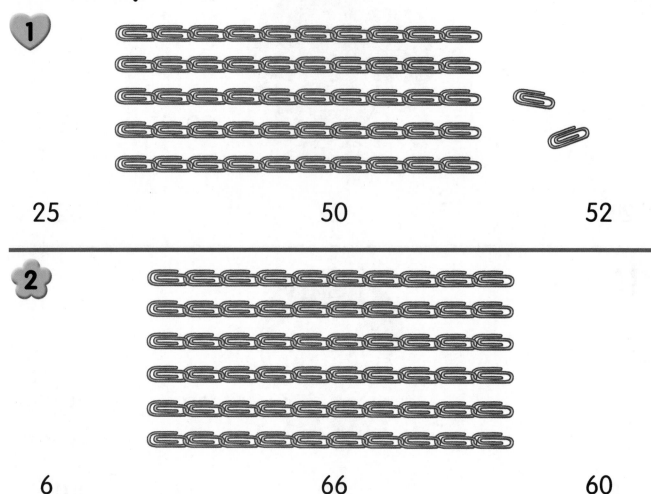

25   50   52

2

66

6   66   60

3

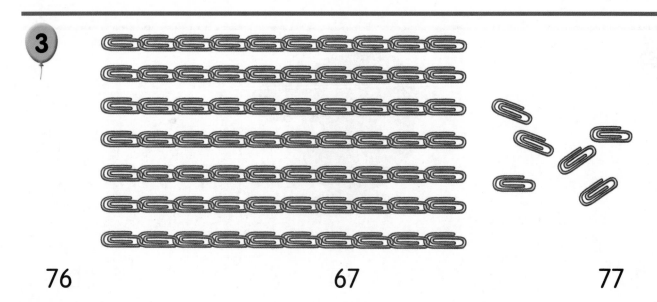

76   67   77

Which is the missing number? Color the balloon.

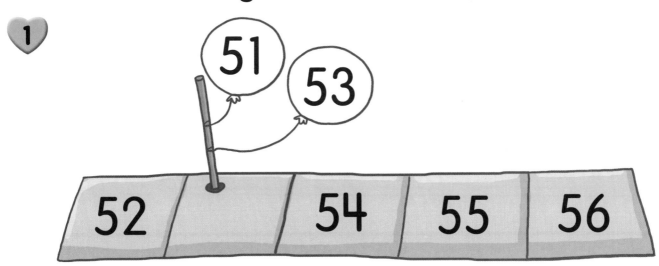

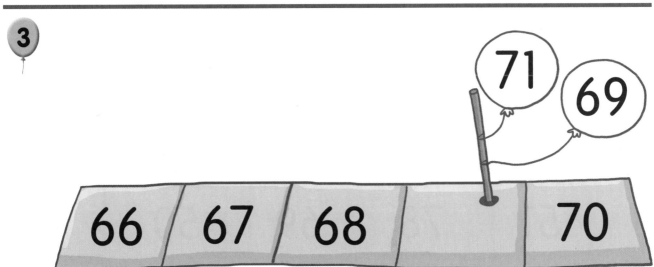

Color the least number orange.
Color the greatest number blue.

 1

| 69 | 72 | 77 | 67 |

2

| 52 | 57 | 51 | 50 |

3

| 79 | 73 | 70 | 60 |

4

| 51 | 78 | 69 | 50 | 71 |

How many? Count and circle.

| 78 | 87 | 88 |

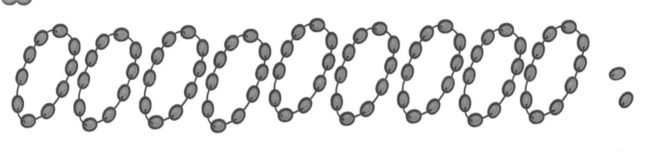

| 90 | 29 | 92 |

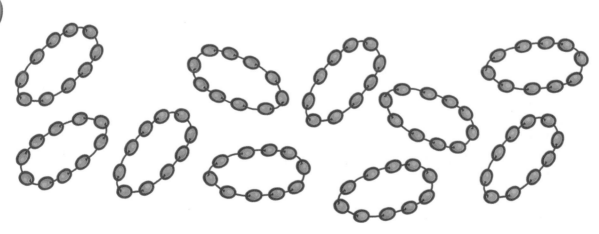

| 80 | 90 | 100 |

Read and color.

 1

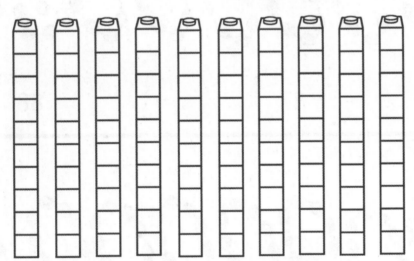

 **2**

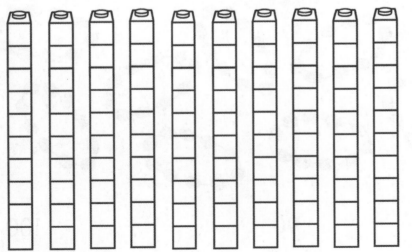

Which is the missing number? Color the flag.

1

85 | 83

80 | 81 | 82 | | 84

2

90 | 91

88 | 89 | | 91 | 92

3

10 | 100

96 | 97 | 98 | 99

What comes before? Color blue.
What comes after? Color red.

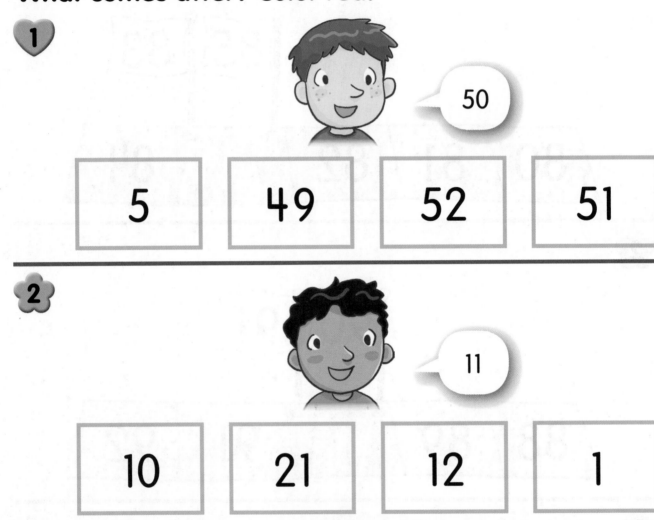

1

50

| 5 | 49 | 52 | 51 |

2

11

| 10 | 21 | 12 | 1 |

3

99

| 79 | 100 | 89 | 98 |

9 Comparing Sets

Lesson 1 Comparing Sets of Up to 10

Count and write.

 1

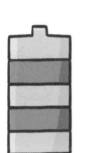 

 2

 3

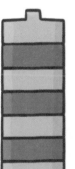 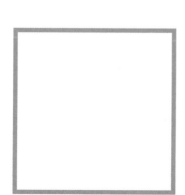

 4

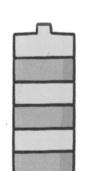 

Which has more? Color.
Which has fewer? Circle.

 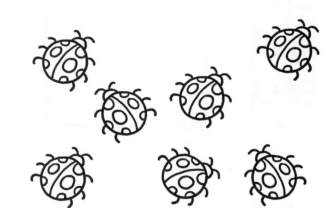

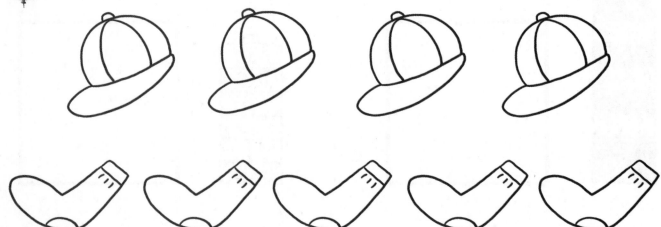

What cannot be counted? Circle.

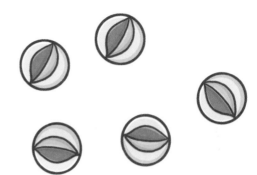

FLOUR

Count and write.
Circle the set with more.

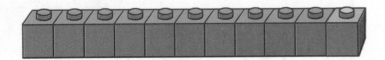

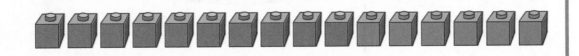

Match one-to-one.
Then, color the set with fewer.

 1

2

3

Lesson 3 Comparing Sets to Find the Difference

Color the extra cubes red.
Count and write how many more.

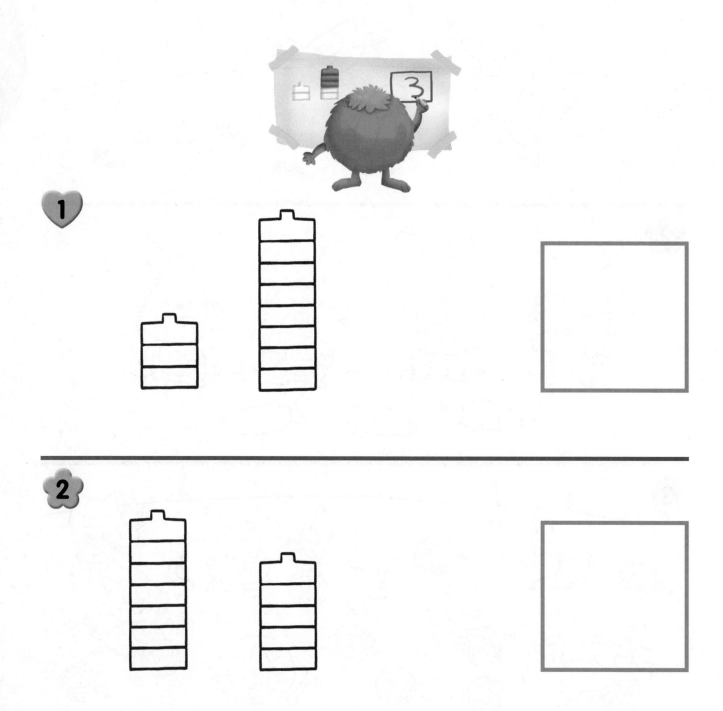

1

2

Draw, count, and write.

Draw a tower of 3 cubes in Box A.

Draw a tower of 5 cubes in Box B.

Box A

Box B

The tower in Box A has _____ fewer cubes than the

tower in Box B.

2

Draw 14 cubes in Box C.

Draw 11 cubes in Box D.

Box C   Box D

Box C has _____ more cubes than Box D.

Lesson 4 Combining Sets

Count and circle.

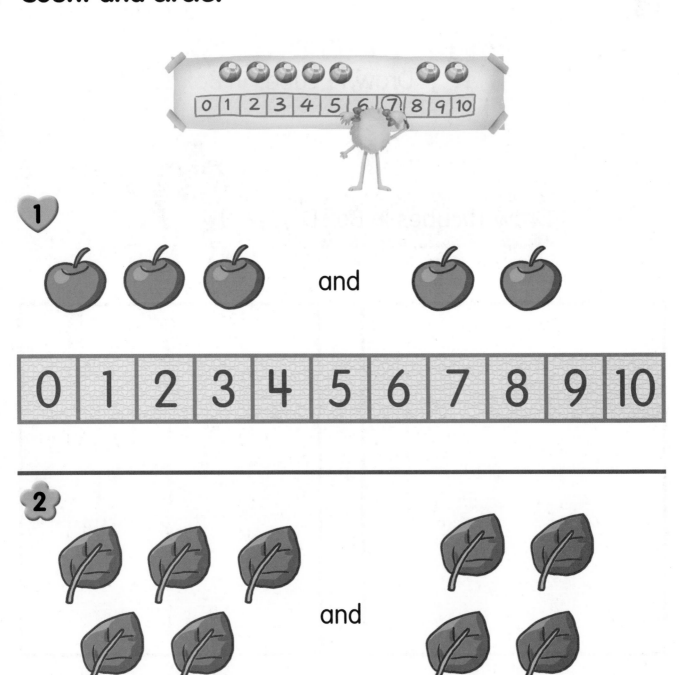

1

      and

0	1	2	3	4	5	6	7	8	9	10

2

      and

0	1	2	3	4	5	6	7	8	9	10

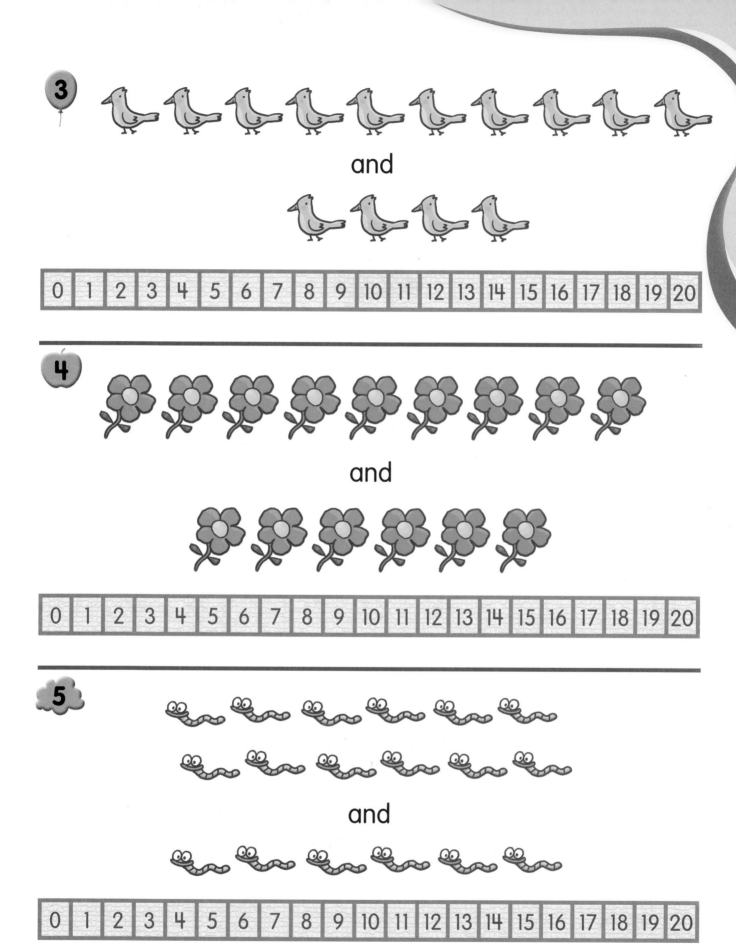

and

0 1 2 3 4 5 6 7 8 9 10 11 12 13 14 15 16 17 18 19 20

and

0 1 2 3 4 5 6 7 8 9 10 11 12 13 14 15 16 17 18 19 20

and

0 1 2 3 4 5 6 7 8 9 10 11 12 13 14 15 16 17 18 19 20

Count, circle, and write.

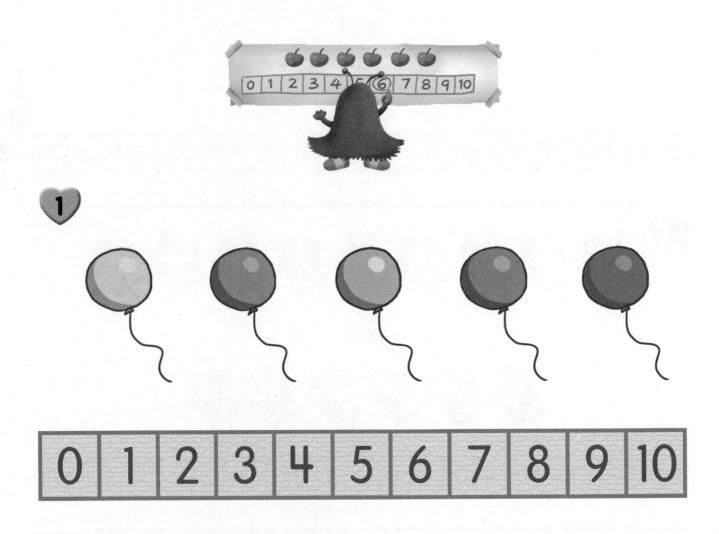

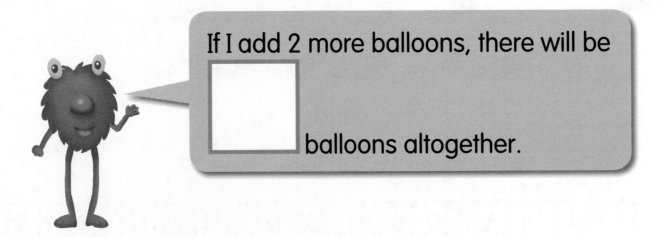

If I add 2 more balloons, there will be

balloons altogether.

2

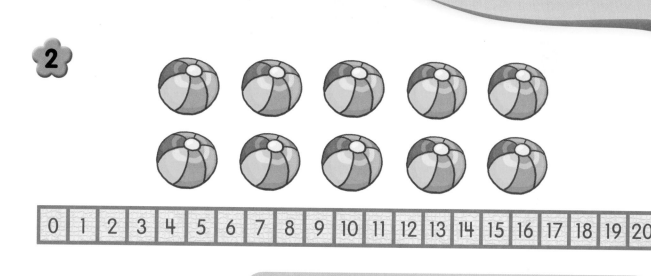

| 0 | 1 | 2 | 3 | 4 | 5 | 6 | 7 | 8 | 9 | 10 | 11 | 12 | 13 | 14 | 15 | 16 | 17 | 18 | 19 | 20 |

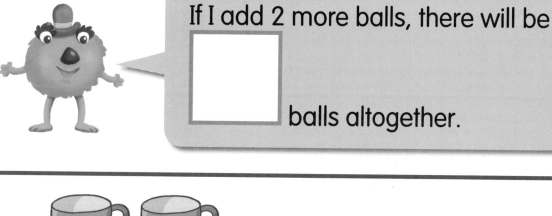

If I add 2 more balls, there will be
[ ]
balls altogether.

3

| 0 | 1 | 2 | 3 | 4 | 5 | 6 | 7 | 8 | 9 | 10 | 11 | 12 | 13 | 14 | 15 | 16 | 17 | 18 | 19 | 20 |

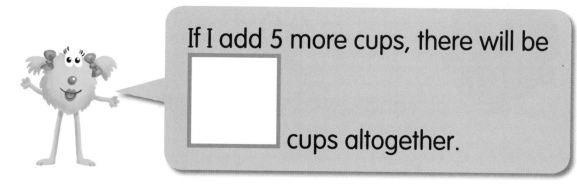

If I add 5 more cups, there will be
[ ]
cups altogether.

Count and write.

 1

 and  is

2

 and  is

3

 and  is

4

17 and  is ☐

5

10 and is ☐

6

19 and is ☐

Lesson 1   Sequencing Events

Pair.

first •

next •

last •

Color the frames.

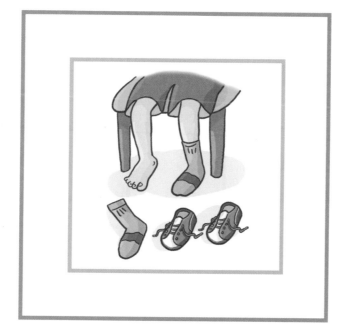

Color.

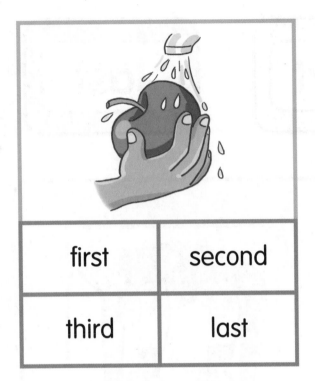

first	second
third	last

first	second
third	last

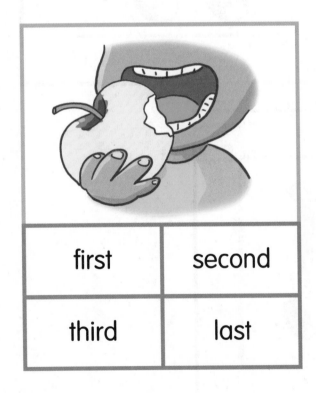

first	second
third	last

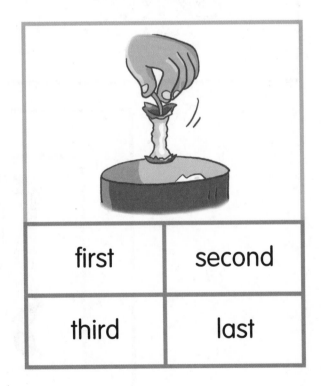

first	second
third	last

Color the child that comes before Baby Bear.
Circle the child that comes after Baby Bear.

Pair.

1st choice •   •

2nd choice •   •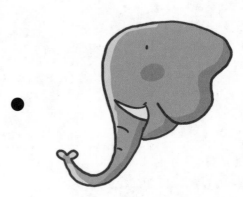

3rd choice •   •

Lesson 1 Days of the Week

What day is it today? Color green.
What day was it yesterday? Color blue.
What day will it be tomorrow? Color yellow.

Sunday		Monday

Tuesday	Wednesday	Thursday

Friday		Saturday

Read and circle.

This day comes after Saturday and before Monday. Which day is it?

Saturday   **Sunday**   **Monday**   **Tuesday**

**Make an X on the month before August.
Circle the month after February. Color the
month between October and December.**

January	February	March
April	May	June
July	August	September
October	November	December

Lesson 1 Counting On to 10

How many more to make 10? Count and write.

1

2

3

4

How many more to make 10? Count and write.

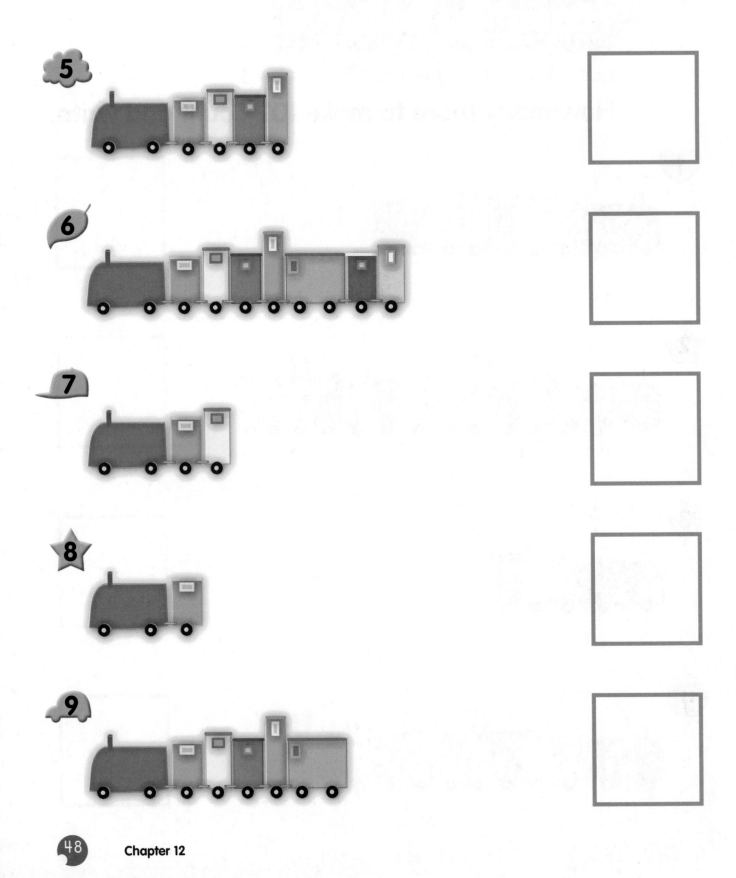

5 ☁

6 🍃

7 🧢

8 ⭐

9 🚗

Lesson 2 Counting Back Using Fingers

Color, count, and write.

1

There are 10 and .

There are 5 , so color 5 .

How many left? _____

How many ? _____

2

There are 10 and .

There are 6 , so color 6 .

How many left? _____

How many ? _____

Color, count, and write.

3

There are 10 and .

There are 3 , so color 3 .

How many left? _____

How many ? _____

4

There are 10 and .

There are 8 , so color 8 .

How many left? _____

How many ? _____

Lesson **3** Finding Differences Using Fingers

Count, write, and circle.

1

How many ? _____

How many ? _____

Are there more or ?

How many more? _____

Are there fewer or ?

How many fewer? _____

Count, write, and circle.

How many ? _____

How many 🐢? _____

Are there more  or 🐢?

How many more? _____

Are there fewer  or 🐢?

How many fewer? _____

Lesson 1   Repeating Patterns

The objects follow a repeating pattern. Circle the object that comes next.

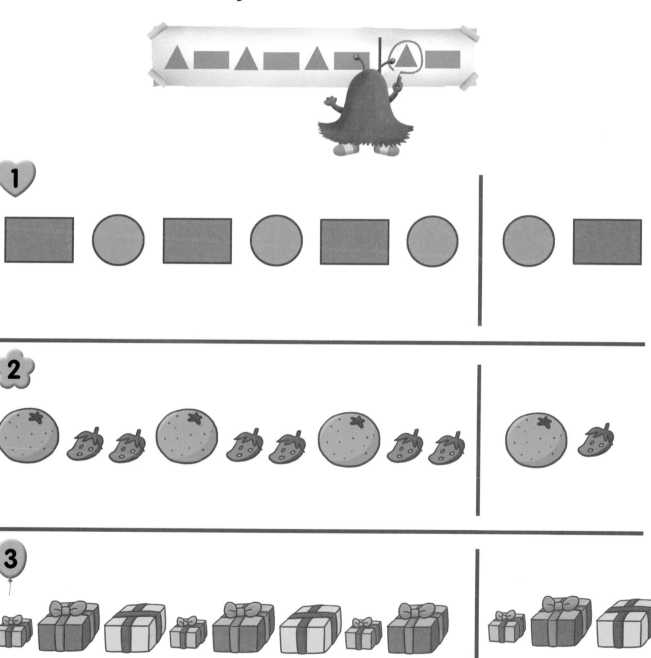

1

2

3

The shapes follow a repeating pattern.
Draw the missing shapes to complete the pattern.

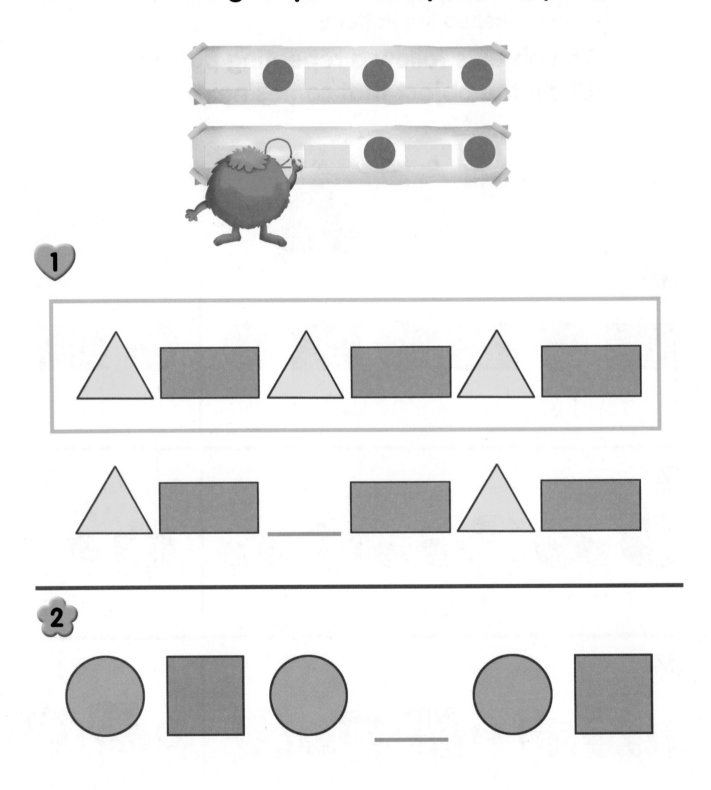

1

2

3

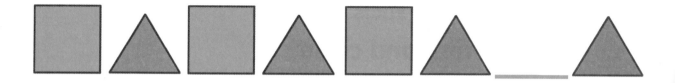

4

5

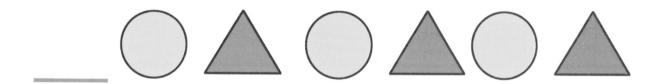

6

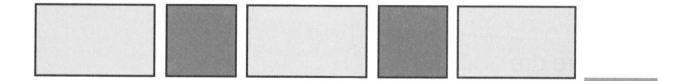

Lesson 1 **Number Facts to 10**

Count, write, and circle.

1

There are _____ .

There are _____ .

How many in all?   2   4   6

2

There are _____ .

There are _____ .

How many in all?   3   6   7

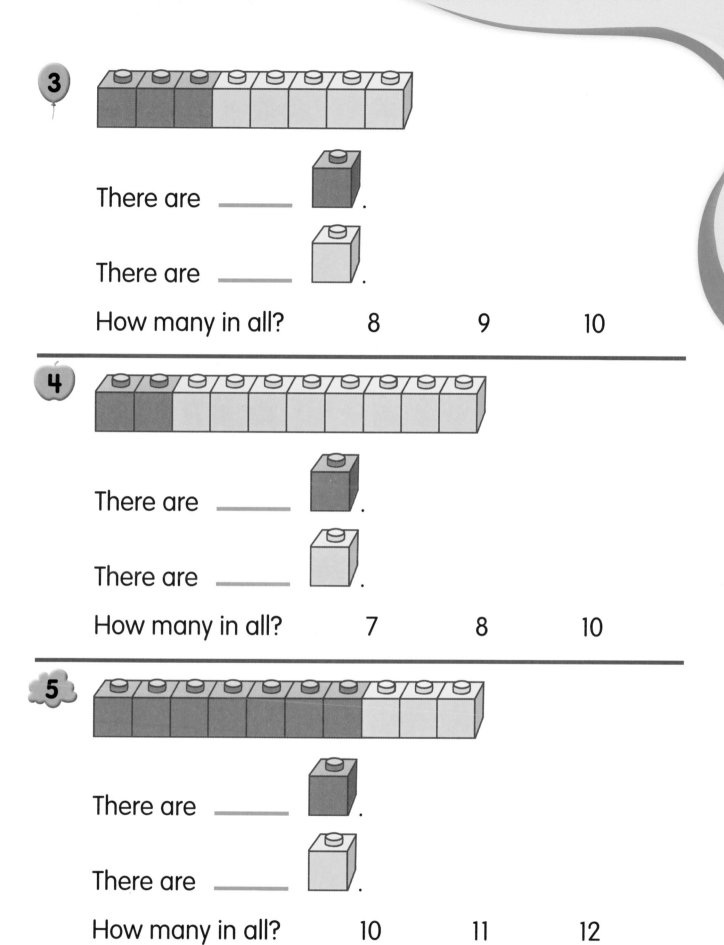

3

There are _____ ▇ .

There are _____ ▢ .

How many in all?   8   9   10

4

There are _____ ▇ .

There are _____ ▢ .

How many in all?   7   8   10

5

There are _____ ▇ .

There are _____ ▢ .

How many in all?   10   11   12

Color, count, and write.
Write the number sentence.

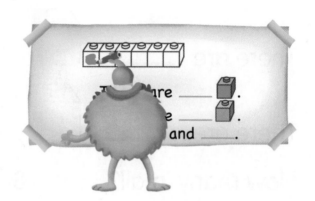

1

There are _____ ⬛ .

There are _____ ⬛ .

5 is _____ and _____ .

2

There are _____ ⬛ .

There are _____ ⬛ .

5 is _____ and _____ .

3

There are _____ 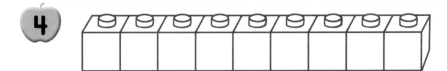.

There are _____ .

7 is _____ and _____ .

4

There are _____ .

There are _____ .

9 is _____ and _____ .

5

There are _____ .

There are _____ .

9 is _____ and _____ .

Lesson 2 Combining Sets

Count and write.

Count how many.
How many more to make 10?

$$\frac{6}{4}$$

 1

Count how many.   _____

How many more to make 10?   _____

 2

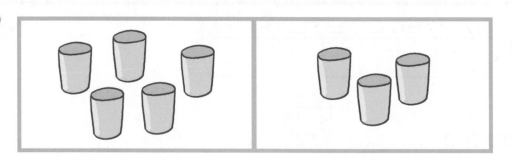

Count how many.   _____

How many more to make 10?   _____

3

Count how many. _____

How many more to make 10? _____

4

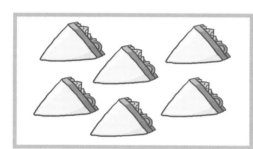 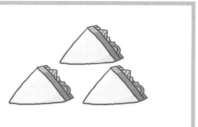

Count how many. _____

How many more to make 10? _____

5

Count how many. _____

How many more to make 10? _____

Count and write. Write the number sentence.

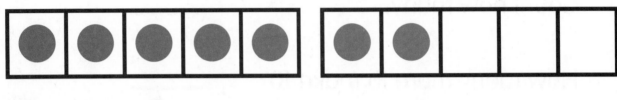

___5___ and ___2___ make _____ .

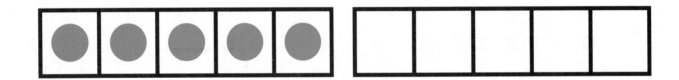

_____ and _____ make _____ .

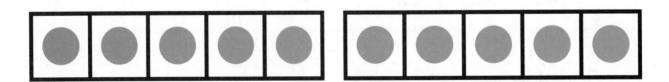

_____ and _____ make _____ .

4

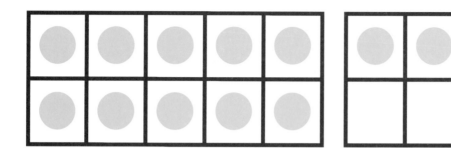

_____ and _____ make _____ .

5

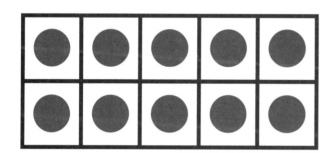 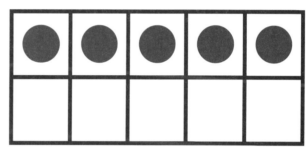

_____ and _____ make _____ .

6

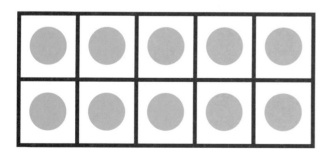 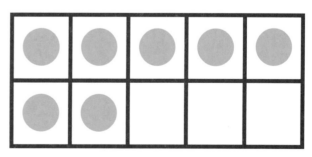

_____ and _____ make _____ .

Draw ◯. Write the number sentence.

1 7

7 is _____ and _____ .

2 9

_____ is _____ and _____ .

3 5

_____ is _____ and _____ .

4

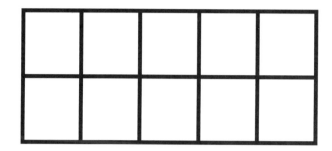 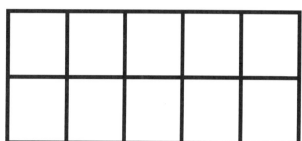

_____ is _____ and _____ .

5

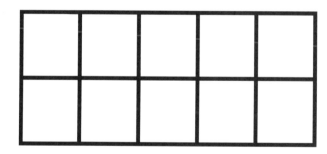 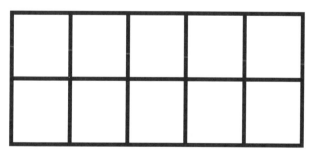

_____ is _____ and _____ .

Count and write.

Count how many.
How many more to make 15?

$\frac{7}{8}$

1

Count how many. _____

How many more to make 15? _____

2

Count how many. _____

How many more to make 15? _____

3

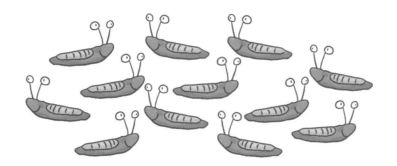

Count how many. _____

How many more to make 15? _____

4

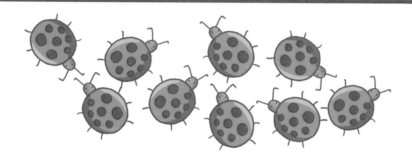

Count how many. _____

How many more to make 15? _____

5

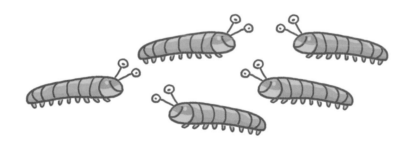

Count how many. _____

How many more to make 15? _____

Count and write.

Count how many.
How many more to make 15?

9
6
15

1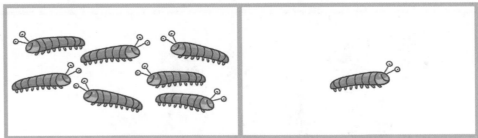

Count how many.   _____

How many more to make 15?   _____

2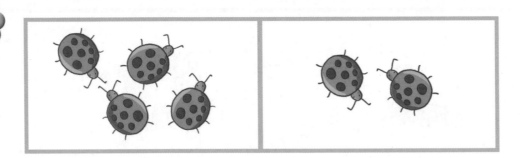

Count how many.   _____

How many more to make 15?   _____

3

Count how many. _____

How many more to make 15? _____

 4

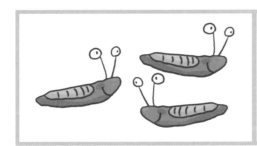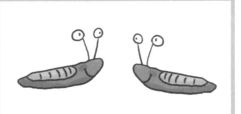

Count how many. _____

How many more to make 15? _____

 5

Count how many. _____

How many more to make 15? _____

WORK MAT

More Fewer